Forex Trading Fundamentals Report 2023

CONTENTS

INTRODUCTION

I hope you have had good years trading. If this is new to you, this will serve as the perfect introduction. For those returning from last year, thank you for your continued support. This year's report is very similar in content; however, it has a predictive essay at the end, which I trust will be worth the price alone.

For those unfamiliar with what I stated last year:

As a person living in a nation that operates under the ideals of individual freedom, I think many people take it for granted that financial transactions are not only allowed but encouraged, to an extent. From what I have observed over the years, many people have made a living from various forms of Forex Trading. I always had an interest in Forex Trading, but when it came to getting a leg-up into the business, I soon realized that it required a great deal of time and a great deal of effort to succeed. So, I thought of doing something different and decided to create a guide to enable people, like myself a few years ago who was trying to get started and have an additional income stream in an unstable world.

I hope this information serves you well.

With times being difficult for many, I have continued to keep this document on sale as low as possible so that it is available for all who wish to make their fortune using Forex.

Will Howell, Albany, New York. 1 April 2023

WHAT IS FOREX?

Forex is a currency marketplace based on the principles of efficient, transparent, and fair trading. The currency market uses online technology for direct communication. The market itself is the platform, and the currency exchange rates on the market are the prices for the real-life exchange rates that trade on the platform. Traders on the market provide liquidity in terms of real-life currency. Traders try to profit from the prices that are posted on the platform. While the platform itself is a medium that trades the money, it is ultimately an arbiter. The arbiter decides who wins and who loses. It does this by considering the demand and supply from the buyers and sellers. Some trades take place on a spot market, with the buyer and seller agreeing upon a date and time for the trade. Other trades are automated by way of algorithms that decide on the price. Some automated trades also display the percentage change of the trading platform, while the others have only percentage information.

The following is some basic terminology to get us started (An additional descriptive glossary is provided at the end of this book):

PIP is the abbreviation of Percentage In Point. This means that for each individual position that is traded, there is a percentage that the buyer needs to pay or the seller needs to receive. If that percentage is not met, then the trade does not go through. The percentage is usually expressed in the following form: X% On or Off. For example, if a position was valued at $30 and the seller wanted to sell it at $30, then the broker would take $30 off the position to give the seller the balance of $25, leaving $10 on the market. This is an indication that the broker is giving the seller a smaller percentage than he would have for the same position without a sell order in place. This is something called liquidity, and the broker has a better and a lesser risk of running out of the position or losing it to an arbiter.

Spread is the cost of making a trade. It is the amount that the broker charges for an order to be processed or executed. In order to reduce this cost, brokers give their clients discounts for either size or quantity. The prices differ for each type of transaction. For example, a buyer would pay a lower price for a larger quantity and a lower price for a smaller quantity. The spread would be the exact size that the buyer wanted for a larger quantity. If the customer wants to get 1,000 shares of Stock A, then the broker would charge him $1000. He could offer 1,000 shares for $2000, and he would charge him $1000 on the trade. The broker is thus taking money from one side to pay for it on the other. Similarly, for a lower quantity, the broker would charge a lower amount for larger quantities.

Margin in Forex is a term used to describe the difference between the amount a trader owes to the broker as an amount of margin or the amount the broker owes to the trader. The difference in the two amounts is what is called the trader's capital or margin.

Premiums are the additional amount that the broker will charge a customer for carrying out an order. When the trader has a small position, the broker would charge the client a small premium, which would also have to be borne by the client. The broker will always charge the client a premium when the client has a small position. In other words, if the trader has 1000 shares and the broker charges him $200 as the premium, then the broker is offering to buy the investor's 1000 shares from him at $200. The buyer of the shares would have to pay the broker this amount for carrying out his order. The broker's premium costs are determined by the seller and by the buyer of the transaction. If both the buyer and the seller agree to the premium, then it would be $200 for the broker's side and $200 for the seller's side.

A commission is an agreed amount which a trader is supposed to pay to the broker when they transact. The commission is charged by the broker and is split equally between the buyer and the seller. The broker is thus paid by both the buyer and the seller. A commission fee is usually between 1.5% and 4.5% of the trading profit of the sale price of the position. In addition to this, the broker would also take a fee for providing services, such as checking the trader's orders and sending a confirmation message. For stocks and options, the broker would charge more commission when a trade is made between two buyers than when the trade is made between two sellers. The total commission charged depends on the amount of the trader's position that he has agreed to buy or sell.

Leverage in Forex means having the ability to trade a large number of shares or amount of money in your account at the same time. Most brokers' margin requirements are based on the customer's net worth. If the customer has $10,000 in the account and has leveraged $10,000 worth of his account, then he needs to be able to trade $20,000 worth of stock or $20,000 worth of money at a time in order to be allowed to continue using the broker's service. A broker would normally allow a client to use his service when he uses less than his net worth. When a broker charges a client for using his service, he usually charges a percentage of the transaction value, which is called the commission.

When a trader has very little money in the account, the broker will be willing to allow a very small amount of leverage. The broker will usually allow a trader who has made a profit on an executed trade to use a broker's service. The broker wants to do this because it gives him an opportunity to make money on the next trade that he facilitates.

Diversification is the practice of making your profits from both long and short trades. This means that you are making money when the stock goes up, and you are losing money when it goes down. A good example of this is with a long position, in which you buy a stock that is down, and then you sell the same stock when it goes back up. The same is true for a short position. You make money when the stock goes down, and you make money when the stock goes up. In a fundamental sense, it is the same with Forex, which is why it is recommended that one have a certain percentage of one's trading account in long and short trades.

Open interest is the number of open contracts of the trader at a particular time. The open interest is shown in the final line of the exchange data, before the current time, so that one can get an idea of the amount of positions that exist in the account. The open interest is a leading indicator for the direction of the market.

Let us first discuss the types of Forex traded on the platform, starting with the most basic type of Forex.

1. For an Individual Person:

This is the simplest form of trading, and it is the type that the average person uses to make money. The seller supplies money to the buying party on the market, and in return, the buying party is given something that can be exchanged into cash on the market. One benefit of this type of trading is that a person may make money if the currency's market value rises.

2. For Large groups to Trade with:

Large groups of individuals may decide to trade with each other in this type of Forex. The traders may choose to have the trading platform send them cash because the traders have not purchased the currency directly.

TYPES OF FOREX

L et us first discuss the types of Forex traded on the platform, starting with the most basic type of Forex.

1. For an Individual Person:

This is the simplest form of trading, and it is the type that the average person uses to make money. The seller supplies money to the buying party on the market, and in return, the buying party is given something that can be exchanged into cash on the market. One benefit of this type of trading is that a person may make money if the currency's market value rises.

2. For Large groups to Trade with:

Large groups of individuals may decide to trade with each other in this type of Forex. The traders may choose to have the trading platform send them cash because the traders have not purchased the currency directly.

Predictive and Regular Signals in Forex

When it comes to the type of signals used in Forex, they can be classified in two ways. They can either be predictive or regular signals. The two types of signals are used to give traders information and direction as to which currency to use. However, there are very different ways that a trader can benefit from using both types of signals.

Predictive signals

The first type of signal is the regular signal which is the type of signal that traders are used to. For example, when a prominent trader uses the regular signal, traders also know that the trader will make a profit when they use the currency in the future. In other words, the regular signal is the regular price signal that traders can use. In the same way, the first type of signal also uses a formula that traders can use to work out the probability of a price movement.

However, the regular signal is not as common as the predictive signals. The latter is considered a better signal as it gives the trader a lot of information at once. The regular signal does not provide any information to the traders. On the other hand, the predictive signal is exceptionally accurate, making the trader work out what will happen in the near future with a lot of ease. However, the signals provided by the platform should be used to their full potential for the trader to make the most of them.

By knowing the probability of a move, the trader can use it as a counter. By knowing that a big trader will take a specific currency, the trader can then use the predictors to ensure they follow the trader's move.

Trading Forex is not just a field for big traders; it is a serious form of trading that requires enormous skill and dedication from the trader. The types mentioned above of signals are just some of the ways that big traders use to play the Forex market to the best of their abilities.

In most countries, including the United States, the language used is English. In the United States, English is not the first language, which is why Forex traders are referred to as Speculators.

If you would like to become a Forex Trader and make money, it is best to find out as much information about the Forex market as possible. The best Forex traders learn as much as they can about the Forex market, and then they try to find the best ways that they can use to make money from the market. The best Forex trading firms have all the information that you need.

The Forex market is extremely popular, and the Forex trading profession does not involve many risks. The Forex market allows traders to earn money with almost no risk. The risks that a trader is exposed to are almost always small. The significant risks that a trader is exposed to are just the market movements.

Many experienced Forex traders will tell you that the Forex market offers good returns at very low risk. The Forex market has been around for a long time, and it has been hugely successful. It is highly likely that the Forex market is here to stay.

Currency Instruments

What is a Currency Instrument?

The Forex currency instrument is a type of currency exchanged in a foreign currency. The currency traded in Forex is not the same as the currency held in the country. In other words, a country's currency can trade against the currency that is traded in the Forex market.

The currency traded in Forex is referred to as the Currency Instrument. Currency instruments are currency that are bought and sold. The Forex market can also trade currency that is not traded in the market. For example, currency that is traded on the stock market cannot be traded in the Forex market.

Currency Instruments are traded using three different methods. Traders can trade Currency Instruments by using the following methods:

Type of Currency Instruments

1. The Comparison Method

Currency instruments can be traded using the Comparison Method. This means that a trader will try to buy the currency with the highest price. This will maximize his profit in the long run.

2. The Market Making Method

Currency instruments can also be traded using the Market Making Method. This means that the trader will try to sell the currency trading at the lowest price and buy the currency trading at the highest price. This will minimize his losses in the long run.

3. The Purchase Method

Currency instruments can also be traded using the Purchase Method. This means that the trader will buy the currency that is trading at the lowest price. This will maximize his profits in the long run.

The difference between the two methods mentioned above is that the Market Making Method does not take into account the amount of profit that the trader is losing to the amount of profit that he is earning. The Market Making Method tries to maximize profit. This means that a trader using the Market Making Method will lose money that he is earning in a situation where he has to sell currency.

Risk is a key concept when it comes to the Forex market. A trader that uses the Comparison Method is taking a lot of risk in the long run. He is taking the risk of buying a currency that is trading at the highest price and then trying to sell it at the lowest price. The worst-case scenario is that he would have to sell a currency for much less than it is worth.

The buyer of currency using the Market Making Method is taking the most risk. He is taking the risk of buying a currency that is trading at the lowest price and then trying to buy it at the highest price.

Currency instruments are traded using the Comparison Method and the Market Making Method.

The Market Making Method requires a lot of risk in the long run. If the trader cannot accurately predict the level of the currency in which the currency is traded, he will be losing a lot of money in the long run. A trader using the Market Making Method will not see the highest profit in the long run because he has to place a large amount of money to make his trades.

How to Get Started in Forex

Investing in Forex.com is a straightforward process. The first thing a trader needs to do is create an account on the company's website. The next step that the trader has to take is to get a large sum of money that he will need to make the trades. The final step is to start buying the currency and selling the currency.

The choice of the currency that a trader buys and sells is critical. The trader needs to make sure that the currency that he is trading is one that he can make money on. There are different methods that the trader can use to make sure that he makes money trading in the Forex market. The most popular method is by having a good knowledge of the market. The traders will then be able to buy and sell the currency with great success.

Community

If there is a trader that knows how to trade Forex, the trader will often contact him or her. If the trader is still new to Forex, he will be looking for a trader to learn the ropes of the currency. The trader will want to learn about the market, and the currency, in which the trader will be trading. The trader will look for a teacher that can teach him how to trade. Many teachers that teach the trader the basics of Forex will get paid for their services. The teacher will make a good amount of money in the long run because the trader will be coming back to him with significant profits that he will be able to use.

Cryptocurrency Trading

Cryptocurrency trading is a very popular trading method. The trader will have to use special software in order to trade in the cryptocurrency. The software is very easy to use, and it is very convenient for the trader. The trader will also need to invest a lot of time learning the cryptocurrency and profit from it. The trader will also have to use many different strategies to make the cryptocurrency. The trader will need to invest a lot of money to make his first profit from cryptocurrency trading. The trader will also be more vulnerable to losing money in the long run. If the trader can make a lot of money with cryptocurrency trading, he will often go out of his way to learn more about it.

What is a Forex Broker?

When a trader has to find a Forex broker, they will look for a company that offers a variety of products. Some of the Forex broker's products are foreign currencies, CFDs, spread betting, and many other services that are common in the market. When a trader needs to find a Forex broker, the trader must do a lot of research before choosing the broker they will choose. The trader should look for a company that is trusted and which is seen as being reputable in the market. The trader should also look for a company that can provide a high level of customer service.

A Forex broker is not just a broker that offers currency trading. The Forex broker is often seen as a trader itself. The trader will often look for a broker that is also a trader. The trader will look for a broker that can provide him with a good level of service. The trader will look for a Forex broker that is seen as being reliable and which is seen as being trustworthy.

Forex Trading Times/Trading Sessions

The regular forex trading times depend on your territory. For example, the international currency trading times depend on what currency you are trading. The trading sessions for the currency differ according to the currency. The trading times depend on the currencies that are being traded. When a trader has to make a trade, they will usually look for the best time for the transaction. The most common times for currency trading is during the early hours. When a trader makes a trade, they will need to make sure that the market is open for trading.

When a trader has to trade in the Forex market, he or she will need to make sure that the market is open for trading. When the market is open for trading, the traders need to be in the trade room. The traders will need to be attentive to ensure that the currency is being properly traded. The trader will need to make sure that the market is open and that the traders watch the situation. When the traders are watching the situation, the traders will need to be sure that the currency is trading according to the profit and loss ratio of the currency.

The Forex broker will need to offer different trading hours depending on the currency. For example, if the trader has to trade in the Pound Sterling currency, they will need to trade in the early hours of the day. The most common times to trade in the forex market are during the mornings. When a trader has to trade in the forex market, they will need to be in the trade room during the early hours of the day. The traders will need to be attentive to make sure that the currency is being correctly traded.

How to Make Money in the Forex market

When the Forex market is open, the trader will need to make sure that the prices are being traded according to the profit and loss ratio. The trader will need to watch the market and make sure that the traders are following the pattern of the market. When the traders are following the profit and loss pattern of the market, the trader will need to make sure that the market is open and that the traders are watching the situation. When the traders are watching the situation, the traders will need to be sure that the currency is trading according to the profit and loss pattern of the market.

The trader will need to make sure that the markets are open and that the traders watch the situation. The trader will need to make sure that the market is open and that the traders monitor the status.

Forex Scalping

Scalping is a way to make money in the Forex market. When a trader makes a trade and charges the client, the client will generally ask the trader to make money back. The trader will profit if the client does not ask for his money back. A trader will normally charge the client for doing a good job and will allow the client to make the money back through trading. A trader will normally charge the client for doing a good job and will enable the client to make the money back through trading.

Forex Positional Trading

Positioning can be essential in the Forex market. As a trader, one can position their trades accordingly to create profits in the market. The trader will be able to make more profit if the price of a currency is going up or down. Positioning can be vital; as a trader, one can position their trades accordingly to create profits in the market. The trader will be able to make more profit if the price of a currency is going up or down.

Forex Stop Losses

A stop loss is a trader's loss in a Forex market. A trader will place a stop loss if the market goes up or down. A stop-loss prevents the trader from taking losses in the market.

Pivot Trade in Forex

If you are thinking about moving a trade into profit-making territory, it can help if you understand what a Pivot is. Let us explain it simply and understandably.

A Pivot Trade is where you build a long position in a Forex market to make a profit. You will do this by using a Pivot type Trade Strategy.

The Carry Trade in Forex is just one-way traders can move into the profit-making territory. It is important to keep in mind that this trade involves more risk. It consists in keeping a trading strategy in place while taking on more risk in the market. When the trade takes off, you may not have the option of moving the market back. This is why it is not the best trade to go for right away. But, if you are aware of this risk, it can be a powerful tool. The carry trade in Forex is just one-way traders can move into the profit-making territory. It is essential to keep in mind that this trade involves more risk.

In Summary

Forex trading has a lot to do with psychology.

As a trader, you want to know your chance of succeeding in the market. You will be taking on many risks, which makes it easier to stay out of danger. But, you don't have to be reckless. You need to be cautious when you start trading in the Forex market.

Traders are often seen trading and losing small percentages of their entire accounts. This is simply because traders lack discipline and don't control the risk they take in the market. This can make it easy for a trader to lose small amounts of money. But, small percentage risks in the market can be a powerful tool which can take a trader's trading and profit-making prospects to the next level.

This is just one of the techniques in a trader's arsenal which can help him or her get ahead in the Forex market. The techniques listed in this article are just a few of the many things traders should be aware of when trading.

The real secret to trading in Forex is to find the small movements in the market. This technique can help you find patterns in the market which can be profitable. The patterns will help you make use of small percentages risks and take advantage of the situation. As you start taking small percentage risks in the Forex market, you will get used to these movements, and you can become an expert trader in time.

To conclude, this is just one of the many ways a trader can benefit from small percentage risks in the Forex market. The techniques mentioned in this report are just a few of the many things learned in the Forex market. The chances of making a profit on small percentage risks in the market are not as high as if you have been trading for a long time. But, as a trader, you should learn about this technique and use it whenever the opportunity arises.

FOREX TRADING IN 2023

I n 2023 it is predicted that with technological advances, how investors trade internationally will change dramatically. For example, by using an instantaneous transaction process via an open exchange, traders can purchase and sell currencies across the globe in real time. This makes the prospect of trading foreign currency in 2023 truly exciting for investors, especially those who are new to trading foreign currency.

On the other hand, trading foreign currency in 2023 will also be affected by the ongoing geopolitical uncertainty and violence in the Middle East region. Investors are worried about the potential implications that political instability could have on the security and stability of international trading. Investors will be concerned about the risks they are exposed to on international trade and more likely to avoid international trades that could expose them to these risks.

Technological advances could also complicate Forex trading in 2023. In the future, investors will have the option to use financial products that could allow them to invest in forex trading. These financial products will allow investors to make trades using different currencies and algorithms to decide the direction of the trading. Therefore, these financial products are most likely used by investors with a proven track record in trading forex.

Interest Rates, Interest Rates and Interest Rates

Interest rates will be the main talking point in 2023. During the 2008 financial crisis, interest rates increased significantly to more than 7% for U.S. treasuries. Since the initial recession, interest rates have decreased back to around the 1% level. This decrease is thanks to the actions of the Federal Reserve. Currently, interest rates are at around 1.8% and are expected to continue to decrease. In 2023 interest rates are predicted to drop to an average of 0.5%, which is significantly lower than in 2023.

In the next five years, interest rates will gradually decrease, and in 2023, interest rates will be reduced to around 0.5%. They could reach zero, where the possibility of negative interest rates comes into play. As interest rates continue to decrease over the next five years, negative interest rates could become possible.

I am personally investing in Forex trading and hope to see a continued increase in the levels of volatility in the forex market. I hope to see interest rates continue to decrease, which will allow investors to purchase financial products such as exchange-traded funds (ETFs) and short-term bonds. These financial products have no strings attached and can be traded in the forex markets and therefore help investors to avoid losses. In 2023 I also hope to see positive returns on my investments from the price volatility of forex. Therefore, I am not worried about being able to accurately predict the future. However, with that caveat, here is how I see the final quarter of 2023 panning out.

The End of 2023

The 2023 markets will end with rising inflation and falling interest rates. Therefore investors should be cautious when purchasing a financial product that has no guarantees in the future. However, investors can invest in forex trading in the coming years if they want to benefit from market volatility and the possibility of negative interest rates in the future.

Be sure to keep an eye on the data, analyze it, keep the risks in the back of your mind and always look to see if the investment suits you before buying. Be prepared to put a lot of money at risk if you decide to invest, as there are many risks when trading internationally.

A Descriptive Glossary of Terms

T o go long is to buy. <u>To go short</u> is to sell. If the price of a currency rises, it is said that <u>the price is up</u>. If the price of a currency falls, it is said that <u>the price is down</u>. If the price of a currency stays the same, it is said to be in a <u>balance</u>. A devaluing currency is one that has gone <u>down in price</u>. A strong currency is one that has <u>increased in price</u>. You can set up a Pivot for both long and short trades.

<u>A Bullish Market</u> is one where the value of the currency goes up. <u>A Bearish Market</u> is one where the value of the currency goes down.

<u>A Moving Average</u> is an indicator that works for both long and short trades. <u>A Major Support Level</u> is the price at which you can buy a currency to create a trade position.

<u>A Major Resistance</u> Level is the price at which you can sell a currency to create a trade position.

<u>A Trendline</u> is a line drawn in the charts representing an established trend in the price of a currency.

A Moving Average Convergence Divergence (MACD) indicates long and short positions. It is used to show momentum in the price of a currency. It gives an indicator of when the price of a currency is likely to move in a particular direction. A Crossover is a line crossed by a currency in the charts. It is an indication that the currency is becoming overbought in one direction and underbought in another direction. It is also an indicator that the price of a currency is

Hawkish and Dovetails are two indicators used to show the potential of a movement in the currency. When a currency is moving towards the Hawkish line, that means it is going to go up. When a currency is moving towards the Dovetail line, that means it will go down. Hawkish and Dovetails are two indicators used to show the potential of a movement in the currency.

Non-Farm Payrolls is a news source that contains information about employment numbers in the United States. Payrolls is a weekly news source that includes information on employment numbers in the United States.

POSSIBILITIES FOR 2023/2024

Possibilities for 2023/2024

Possible Scenario 1: Increased Volatility

The forex market is expected to become more volatile in 2024, driven by global events such as political changes, trade agreements, and economic policies. Investors are likely to shift their focus to emerging markets, which could result in greater volatility in these currencies.

Possible Scenario 2: Rise of Digital Currencies

Cryptocurrencies are expected to gain more mainstream adoption in 2024, potentially disrupting the traditional forex market. This could result in increased volatility as investors try to balance the risks and rewards of investing in these digital assets.

Possible Scenario 3: Continued Growth of Forex Trading

Despite the challenges posed by geopolitical and economic uncertainties, the forex market is expected to continue its growth trajectory in 2024. This is due to the increasing number of retail traders and the rise of algorithmic trading, which has made forex trading more accessible and cost-effective.

Possible Scenario 4: Greater Regulation

Regulatory authorities around the world are expected to continue tightening their oversight of the forex market in 2024. This could lead to greater transparency and accountability, but it could also result in higher compliance costs for forex brokers and traders.

Overall, the forex market in 2024 is likely to be shaped by a combination of global events, technological advances, and regulatory changes. To succeed in this environment, traders will need to stay informed and adaptable, using the latest tools and strategies to manage their risk and maximize their returns.

FINAL THOUGHTS

In conclusion, the forex market is constantly evolving, and predicting its future can be a challenging task. Based on current trends and historical data, we can make some educated guesses about what might happen in 2023.

Increased volatility is a likely scenario due to global events such as political changes, trade agreements, and economic policies. Additionally, the rise of digital currencies could potentially disrupt the traditional forex market and lead to greater volatility. However, despite these challenges, the forex market is expected to continue its growth trajectory in 2023 due to the increasing number of retail traders and the rise of algorithmic trading.

Furthermore, regulatory authorities are expected to continue tightening their oversight of the forex market in 2023, which could lead to greater transparency and accountability.

To succeed in the forex market in 2023, traders will need to stay informed and adaptable, using the latest tools and strategies to manage their risk and maximize their returns. Additionally, traders should consider diversifying their portfolios and hedging their positions to mitigate potential losses in case of unexpected events.

Good luck, as always.

Will Howell

Notes

NOTES

www.ingramcontent.com/pod-product-compliance
Lightning Source LLC
Chambersburg PA
CBHW071124220526
45467CB00004B/2061